PONDERING THE LABYRINTH

PONDERING THE LABYRINTH

Questions to Pray on the Path

JILL KIMBERLY HARTWELL GEOFFRION

The Pilgrim Press   Cleveland

They ask me

the most challenging

and therefore the most helpful

questions.

I am grateful.

This book is dedicated to

my husband Tim,

our sons, Tim and Dan,

and my spiritual director, Elizabeth Toohey.

The Pilgrim Press, 700 Prospect Avenue, Cleveland, Ohio 44115-1100
pilgrimpress.com
Copyright © Jill Kimberly Hartwell Geoffrion

The labyrinth illustrations used throughout the book are drawn by Jeff Saward of Labyrinthos. Both the drawings and the accompanying notes are used with his permission.

Biblical quotations, unless otherwise noted, are from the New Revised Standard Version of the Bible, © 1989 by the Division of Christian Education of the National Council of Churches of Christ in the U.S.A., and are used by permission. Alterations have been made to make passages more inclusive. The abbreviation NIV is used for the New International Version.

All rights reserved. Published 2003

Printed in the United States of America on acid-free paper

08   07   06   5   4   3   2

Library of Congress Cataloging-in-Publication Data
Geoffrion, Jill Kimberly Hartwell, 1958–
    Pondering the labyrinth : questions to pray on the path / Jill Kimberly Hartwell
Geoffrion.
        p.   cm.
    Includes bibliographical references.
    ISBN 0-8298-1575-9 (pbk. : alk. paper)
    1. Labyrinths—Religious aspects.   2. Spiritual life.   I. Title.

BL325.L3G46   2003
203'.7—dc22

                                                            2003058039

CONTENTS

With Gratitude

Special thanks to friends who discussed with me the questions and ideas incorporated in this book, including:

Barbara Battin

Linda Campbell

Helen Curry

Cheryl Dudley

Robert Ferré

William Frost

David Gallagher

Tim Geoffrion

Lea Goode

Charlie Hartwell

Lucy Hartwell

Lyndall Johnson

Pamela Johnson

Sally Johnson

Julie McKenzie

Lisa Moriarty

Elizabeth Nagel

Jeff Saward

Kimberly Lowelle Saward

Leeanardi Simpson

Kristine Thompson

INTRODUCTION

We have to start somewhere.
It usually happens long before
the official beginning.

PONDERING THE QUESTIONS

Questions spring naturally from the soil of life. Often they signal that a shift has already begun and point us toward destinations we cannot even imagine. Questions invite growth; sometimes they demand it. At times we welcome questions; at other times they seem to bang on the front door of our lives refusing to leave even when we insist, "I will never, ever let you in!"

Identifying and living with the questions is a critical part of growing. It can be joyful or painful; many times it is both. Well-worded questions can be faithful companions. They can lead through dense thickets of confusion, misunderstanding, fear, and ignorance to open fields where vast horizons of hope, clarity, and wisdom await. Praying the labyrinth with questions is a continuation of my lifelong dialogue with the Sacred. I am curious by nature. When I encounter something I don't understand or can't accept, the questions begin flowing! Being a person of faith, I direct many of my questions to God. The questions that have aided me the most have been those that have allowed for the possibility of change. Whether a shift in knowledge, attitude, physical experience, or spiritual openness is sought, I rely on my questions to the Divine to illuminate the path towards Truth. The questions in this book have done just that; they have directed me towards deeper levels of mental, physical, emotional, and spiritual understanding as I have used them while praying the labyrinth.

Spiritual questions seem to have a preference for circuitous routes. While most school children are trained to look for the one correct answer when a question is posed, those with greater experience discover that many questions are best "answered" not with a statement, but with another question. In the realm of Spirit, questions are more apt to be clues than precursors to obvious solutions. As we pay attention to the questions that emerge from within, we find ourselves moving away from secure shores into what appear to be uncharted waters. Sometimes we panic; sometimes we trust. Either way, the questions, once identified, wait for us to engage them seriously.

Labyrinths, winding pathways that double back once or many times before reaching a center, provide a wonderful haven where questions can be welcomed, honored, and explored. Sometimes the questions brought to a labyrinth are answered decisively as one moves within the pattern. Many labyrinth users report that in response to a question, awareness of a related question emerges. Others speak of asking a question before a labyrinth experience, only to discover that they come to understand what is behind the question in new ways. As they move around the labyrinth they become better able to see the question's context from multiple vantage points. Sometimes feelings related to the posed question shift. One labyrinth walker wrote to me, "I realized that God . . . whom I experience profoundly on the labyrinth, has not necessarily answered the questions for me as I've walked, but has made me at peace and comfortable in the midst of questions. Peace through the questions, wow!"

As I facilitate labyrinth events I notice that suggesting focus questions often helps participants frame their explorations in ways they find helpful.

This is no surprise; for many years I have followed a morning ritual of identifying a question to live with throughout that day. Disciplining myself in framing these daily queries has taught me to identify questions that balance focus and openness. I have learned that a few words followed by a question mark create new possibilities in my thinking, feeling, and acting. I have come to appreciate the fact that questions are often invitations in disguise.

The questions you find here have been used by groups as well as individuals; adapt them to fit your situation. It is my hope that these questions will inspire many others!

When combining questions and labyrinths, please remember that choosing a question and then walking a labyrinth pathway to the center and back out may be the most traditional approach, but it's just a start! After identifying a question, it might be more meaningful to gaze at a labyrinth, find one spot on a labyrinth to sit, kneel, or stand for several minutes, walk around the outside, nonjudgmentally watch others as they move, or trace the path of a paper or wooden labyrinth with your finger.

The questions in each chapter have been worded with the potential to offer companionship in differing situations. Use them once or many times!

USING THIS BOOK

Stated simply:

Whatever helps!

Use this book in any way that seems most helpful. Reading it cover to cover makes little sense, but if you look through its pages as if "window shopping" you may spot a treasure that you want to take with you to a labyrinth. Or, after considering the contents page, select a chapter that corresponds to a current need. Consider the questions until one feels engaging or seems timely, then use it as you experience a labyrinth. You may prefer to read through all the questions in a chapter and then wait for one or more to reemerge during a labyrinth experience. Another approach would be to take the book with you as you move on the labyrinth and seek a question as the need arises.

This book is for those who are just learning about the labyrinth as well as for those who have spent significant time with labyrinths. If you are unfamiliar with labyrinths it may be helpful to consult chapter 1, "Frequently Asked Questions about Labyrinths," first.

Chapter 9, "Across Time," offers questions that are meant to stimulate deeper reflection in those who are interested in exploring the potentials of long-term use of labyrinths.

Consider this book an enthusiastic friend who can't help but pose question upon question! Trust that together you can discern what is most helpful and needed. There is plenty of room on each page to write or draw your responses to your labyrinth encounters. A page for your own questions is available at the end of each chapter.

The questions in this book have been carefully worded to nurture your spiritual explorations. Some are predictable. Others will be a surprise. May they all be catalysts for the growth you are seeking.

part one

ABOUT LABYRINTHS

One

FREQUENTLY ASKED QUESTIONS
ABOUT LABYRINTHS

For some,
the need to know "everything"—
or at least more—
is the excuse used
to delay getting started.

For some,
a claimed "lack of interest"
is an irresponsible way
of not making the needed effort to begin.

There is a time to ask,
a time not to ask,
and a time to wait to ask.

What time is it
for you?

WHAT IS A LABYRINTH?

A labyrinth is a symbol,
pattern,
or energy field
that contains a single pathway
that turns back on itself at least once
before leading to a center.

IS THERE JUST ONE LABYRINTH PATTERN?

There are a great number of labyrinth patterns.
Some are ancient; others have been created recently.
The Chartres labyrinth pattern,
which comes from a medieval cathedral in France,
and the Classical or Cretan seven circuit labyrinth pattern
are the two patterns most readily recognized today.

HOW DO MAZES AND LABYRINTHS DIFFER?

Historically the terms "labyrinth" and "maze"
have been used interchangeably.
Now, for the sake of clarity,
distinctions between the two are often employed.
Labyrinths are designed to lead you to a center—
although you turn quite a few times on the way there.
Mazes are designed to confuse
and test your abilities
to solve the difficult challenge of getting to a center.
They incorporate choices that may frustrate your attempts.
Labyrinths do not.

WHAT IS THE PURPOSE OF A LABYRINTH?

There are many.
Different purposes have surfaced throughout history including:
    decoration,

prayer,

protection,

inspiration,

amusement,

guidance,

meditation,

distraction,

creation,

dance,

problem solving,

symbolic reminder of death and rebirth,

psychological exploration,

ritual,

competition involving physical skill,

ceremony.

The list is long and varied.

Labyrinths adapt well to varied purposes.

WHAT IS THE HISTORY OF THE LABYRINTH?

No one is certain of the entire history of the labyrinth. Clues that lead us towards its origins include: a labyrinth doodle on a Greek clay tablet dated 1200 B.C.E.; the older Greek key pattern (also known as the Greek meander pattern) that can be stretched into a labyrinth; the orbit of Mercury as observed from Earth; and mythological stories such as the one involving Theseus and the Minotaur.

We know that over time labyrinths of various shapes and sizes have appeared on every inhabited continent.

Jeff Saward, labyrinth historian, identifies six periods of labyrinth flowering in western cultures. He notes that each of these was marked by rapid change:

The Bronze Age

The Roman Period (150 B.C.E.–350 C.E.)

The Medieval Period (roughly 800 C.E., peaking in the 1200s)
The Renaissance Period (1500–1600s)
The Victorian Period (mid- to late 1800s)
The Current Period (beginning in the late 1960s and continuing)

WHY ARE SO MANY LABYRINTHS BEING BUILT NOW?

This period of interest in and use of labyrinths
may be a response to constant social change,
the desire for spiritual experiences
that are not mediated by a religious authority,
or a symbolic expression of a widespread desire
for the balancing of rationality and creativity.
Perhaps the answer involves a combination of all these suggestions
as well as others that will become clearer over time.

WHY WOULD SOMEONE USE A LABYRINTH?

To gain clarity.
To break old patterns.
To explore.
To connect with God.
To receive help.
To become more open.
To relax.
To find wisdom.
To celebrate.
To turn a new corner.
To pray.
To integrate inner and outer realities.
To heal.
To wonder.
To see if anything is going to happen.
To meditate.
To connect with Sacred Truth.

BEFORE USING A LABYRINTH, WHAT DOES A PERSON NEED TO KNOW?

Nothing.

Many suggest that experiencing a labyrinth
is the best introduction possible.

Willingness to engage the pattern
and be engaged by the pattern
is all that is needed.

IS THE LABYRINTH ASSOCIATED WITH ANY PARTICULAR RELIGIOUS TRADITION?

Throughout history labyrinths have been used
by members of many spiritual and secular traditions
for differing purposes.
Some labyrinth patterns have been altered or created
to include specific religious messages,
such as the addition of the cross shape
within some Christian labyrinths.
Because of the symbolic nature of labyrinths,
they are open to varying interpretations.
Therefore, people of different religious backgrounds
are able to be together on a labyrinth
in ways that are spiritually meaningful,
but do not always carry the same content.

IS IT SAFE FOR ME TO TRY THIS SPIRITUAL TOOL?

The labyrinth is a safe space.
If at any time you want to,
you can simply walk off the pattern.

WHAT IS THE CORRECT WAY TO USE A LABYRINTH?

However you feel ready
to the engage the labyrinth
is the "right" way to use it.

Because there are an unlimited number of ways to use a labyrinth,
you may want to enter the pattern
and allow your intuition to guide you.
Or, you may wish to follow the path to the center and back out.
It may be more compelling to gaze at the pattern.
One can have a labyrinth experience by witnessing others inside
while remaining outside.
A person can walk on and off a labyrinth at will;
it is okay and sometimes advisable to go to the center
without taking the pathway.
Walking around the outside of the labyrinth can be as valuable
as walking around its inside.
Perhaps you will want to go to a particular place on the labyrinth
where you will sit, kneel, or stand.
The possibilities are limitless.
Choose one that seems most useful;
let your needs guide your decisions.

WHAT IS INVOLVED IN A TYPICAL LABYRINTH WALK?

A typical contemporary way of walking a labyrinth involves:
Preparing,
Crossing the threshold,
Following the path to the center,
Spending time there,
Using the same path to return to the threshold,
Crossing the threshold,
Allowing the experience to flow into your life.

Atypical ways of encountering the labyrinth
can be even more meaningful!

WHAT SHOULD A PERSON DO IF HE OR SHE IS ON THE PATH BUT DOESN'T WANT TO FOLLOW IT ALL THE WAY BACK TO THE THRESHOLD?

You may walk off the pattern at any time.
Almost all labyrinths have no hedges
or other barriers that would keep a walker from leaving.
Just as you can walk off the labyrinth when you want,
you can also walk to any point on a labyrinth
and begin your encounter from there.
Following the path in to the center and back out to the threshold
is a traditional approach used by many people today;
other options can be equally beneficial!

CAN A PERSON GET LOST ON A LABYRINTH?

There is only one path that leads to the center
(and, if taken, that returns a walker to the threshold)
so as long as you stay on the path you can't get "lost."

Sometimes people step off the path and get turned around.
If this happens to you,
you will either end up in the center or at the threshold.
You can then decide
whether or not your labyrinth experience is complete.

Sometimes it is; sometimes it's not.

WHAT LABYRINTH ETIQUETTE EXISTS?

Consideration for self and others
is the cornerstone of labyrinth etiquette.

Staying with your pace is important,
even as it changes during a single walk.
It's okay to walk around others or to let them walk around you.

Some labyrinth experiences happen in silence;
others don't.

Allowing your encounter with a labyrinth to unfold naturally
seems to be the most helpful guideline.

HOW DOES THE LABYRINTH "WORK" IN CREATING THE SHIFTS THAT PEOPLE DESCRIBE?

No one is sure.
Some theorize that the motion of turning back and forth
balances the activity of both hemispheres of the brain and creates shifts
such as feeling more relaxed or peaceful, gaining insights, or a deepening of
spiritual commitments.

Others write that labyrinths are archetypal forms with their own power.

It has been suggested that because people come to labyrinths
with an expectation that something is going to "happen," it does.

Those who have studied sacred geometry
believe that the proportions of the patterns communicate
so that people feel a connection to their Creator.

While we wait for scientists and others to investigate more fully,
we must admit we don't know.

Fortunately, mysteries don't have to wait for full comprehension before
bestowing their gifts!

WHAT IF NOTHING HAPPENS WHEN I EXPERIENCE A LABYRINTH?

Just wait.

The labyrinth may offer gifts that are not immediately obvious.

Many people find that the meanings of a labyrinth encounter
do not become fully evident for days, weeks, or even months.

Sometimes people sense that something profound is happening,
but initially they cannot externalize
the meanings of their experience with words.

Questions I would like answered

*Constructed from wave-rolled rocks
in the early 1700s, the Troy Town labyrinth
still survives on the remote island of St. Agnes,
off the southwest coast of England.*

part two

QUESTIONS TO PONDER
AS YOU EXPERIENCE
THE LABYRINTH

Two

P R E P A R I N G

Beware!

Setting off on an adventure
often begins innocently enough.

What is drawing me toward a labyrinth?

What fears
are standing between the labyrinth and me?
Am I willing to greet them
and ask them to move out of the way?

I've heard about labyrinths;
what plans do I need to make so I can experience one?
What prayers
are longing for expression
through my use of the labyrinth?

Do I want to experience the labyrinth alone
or with others?
Is there someone else whom I would like to invite
to experience the labyrinth with me?

What will help me prepare
for my labyrinth experience?

What possibilities are begging for exploration?

How can I gather sufficient courage
to take that first step on a brand new path?

My questions

*Situated on the crown of a steep hillside,
overlooking the confluence of three major rivers, the
Julian's Bower turf labyrinth at Alkborough on the east
coast of England is probably late medieval in origin.*

Three

BEFORE CROSSING THE THRESHOLD

There are times
when we are neither here
nor there.

Imagine a world where
we honored transitions enough
to take at least a moment
to notice and acknowledge them.

Why have I come?

What hungers
are leading me to seek nourishment
at a labyrinth?

What are the desires of my heart?

Which symbolic gestures
express best my hopes for this time?

What do I bring to this experience?

Am I open to change?

If the internal or external resistance
I am experiencing had a voice,
what would it say?
What responses do I want to make?

How might my breath
and the labyrinth work together
for my good?

If I were to create a banner
that I would carry during my labyrinth experience
as an outward sign of my inner intentions,
what would it be like?

How do I want to move on the labyrinth today?
What might hold me back?
What will help me to feel free to express myself fully?

Would it be more helpful
to spend time gazing at the labyrinth,
walking around its perimeter,
or moving on it?

Is there someone
to whom I would like to dedicate this walk?

What intentions will I embodying
as I move on the labyrinth?

What will I leave outside the labyrinth?

What will I bring into the labyrinth with me?

What am I waiting for?

My questions

*A labyrinth carved on a stone in the royal palace
at Bhaktapur, Nepal, was said to represent the
defenses of the legendary city of Scimangada.*

Four

BETWEEN THE THRESHOLD AND THE CENTER

Don't accept these messages:

"You're doing this wrong!"
"You are going to get lost."
"You shouldn't have come."
"This isn't going to work."

Welcome these messages:

"I am on a life-affirming path."
"I'm being led to the Center."
"Something important is being set in motion."
"I can pay attention to what is happening around and within me."

What do I need?

Where am I heading?

How am I finding my way?

What am I becoming aware of?

What path am I on?

Where are my explorations taking me?

What needs to be released?

What am I learning?

Where will my next step take me?

How is my story changing?

How am I responding
to the invitations I am receiving
to let go?

What am I being taught?

What do I hear when I listen
to the voice of my steps?

Is my pace helping me?
Would it be more useful to slow down?
To speed up?
To stop?
To get moving?

Who is here with me?

How can the turns of the labyrinth
help me explore experiences of turning
I'm going through?

When I wonder
"Will this path really take me to the center?"
what thoughts come next?

Where are my longings leading?

What possibilities are forming as I move along this path?

How does my body want to pray as it moves on this pattern?

What is moving through me?

What emotions travel with me on this path?

What do I want to communicate to the fears
I am encountering?

Am I going with or against the flow?
What if I allowed the flow to move me?

What words and phrases are bubbling up inside?

What sounds is the labyrinth evoking?

If I were to meet a mythical creature right now,
what would it communicate to me?

What needs to move?

What is dropping away
as I weave my way towards the center?

What is dying?

What perceptions are becoming clearer?

Am I there yet!?!?

Do I want to continue?

My questions

Collected in 1935, in the remote Gran Chaco region
of Brazil, this drawing of a labyrinth by a Caduveo native
raises interesting questions concerning the occurrence
of the labyrinth in South America.

Five

IN THE CENTER

Sigh.

Deep sigh.

Deeper sigh.

Deepest sigh yet!

What am I experiencing?

How might I become more open to the love that surrounds and even envelops me?

Why am I here?

How am I joined with others (from my past or present) in the center?

What is my body communicating?

Will tears be a welcome part of this experience? Will laughter?

What is being drawn up from the well of intuition?

What am I smelling? How are these scents inviting me to pray?

How will I signal my intention to let go of my resistance?

What postures or positions will help me accept the invitation to rest?

What is flowering in the center of my life?

What do I need to know, understand, or see?

Where am I most at home?

In what ways is this center empty? In what ways is this center full?

Based on the experience of this moment, how would I answer the question, "What is eternal?"

If a musician suddenly materialized here in the center, what instrument would she or he be playing? What would I hear?

What lies beneath the surface, deeper than appearances?

What sacred communications am I aware of right now?

If an angel were to join me here, what message would it bring?

Am I ready to move on?

My questions

*Laid in black and white marble in 1870, the labyrinth
in Ely Cathedral in Eastern England is typical of the
labyrinths created in churches and cathedrals across
Europe in the late nineteenth century.*

Six

BETWEEN THE CENTER AND THE THRESHOLD

Here I go again!

Why does it feel like I've never been here before?

What, if anything, have I left in the center?

What movements best express my feelings?

If my pace had a voice, what would it be telling me?

As I encounter others, how do I want to move?

Am I on the way out or the way in—or both?

What is inviting my "Yes!"?

What do I sense is in front of me, even though I can't see it?

Is a particular word or image coming into my awareness?

From inside the labyrinth, what do I notice about what is outside?

What is being resurrected?

What changes are possible?

Where am I headed?

Is there a phrase that is comforting or challenging me as I move?

What barriers am I perceiving on the path?

What am I learning? Why does it matter?

Who can help me?

What thoughts are moving in and through me?

What am I circling? What is encircling me?

What do I need to accept?

What do I most want?

What am I being invited to be or do?

My questions

The famous pavement labyrinth in
Chartres Cathedral, France, created during the
first few years of the thirteenth century, is one
of the finest surviving examples of its type.

Seven

BEFORE EXITING THE THRESHOLD

One foot here,
One foot there.

Where am I?

What has been given and received?

In what ways is this an ending? In what ways is it a beginning?

Where am I heading?

What truths have become clearer?

What awareness does my body have?

What obstacles have I encountered?

Where do I want to go next?

What have I left behind?

What is waiting?

Am I ready to move on?

My questions

*This labyrinth pattern, from a design copybook
carried by a wandering Korawa tattooist in southern
India, was collected during the 1930s.*

part three

QUESTIONS TO PONDER AWAY FROM THE THE LABYRINTH

Eight

SOON AFTER

Breathe in for one count.
Breathe out for two counts.

Breathe in for two counts.
Breathe out for four counts.

Breathe in for three counts.
Breathe out for six counts.

Now breathe normally
While focusing on who you are in this moment.

Once you are here,
You are ready to revisit where you have been.

Where have I been?

What happened on the labyrinth? What happened inside me?

What gifts of wisdom were shared?

If the labyrinth had a voice, what would it say about the time we just spent together?

What has been revealed?

What words, symbols, feelings, or sounds best express what occurred?

What needs to be clarified?

Am I experiencing a call to action or waiting?

What are the most important messages of my labyrinth experience?

What is the significance of what I have just learned?

How can I continue to explore and enjoy the gifts I have received?

Would it be most helpful to talk about my labyrinth experience or to keep silent for now?

What expressions of gratitude do I want to offer?

What discoveries do I need to spend more time with?

Is there someone that I want to invite to experience a labyrinth?

Do I want to continue this experience by entering the labyrinth again?

My questions

Formed from 2,401 square paving stones,
the labyrinth formerly occupying the south transept
of the Abbey of St. Bertin in St. Omer, France, was
of a unique design and nearly thirty-six feet wide.

Nine

ACROSS TIME

Recipe for Depth

Take several experiences,
some skepticism,
a pinch of humor,
intermittent pondering,
a little amazement,
a well-worded question,
one heart opened as widely as possible,
and willingness to think carefully.

Mix as thoroughly as you can.
Let sit for a good amount of time.

Uncover.
Use whatever awaits!

Why do I use labyrinths?

What is it about the labyrinth that promotes such deep reflection and prayer?

Why not just go on a walk outdoors and turn around a few times?

Can I identify any patterns in my life (situations, emotions, thoughts) that draw me towards labyrinths?

Is there a simple prayer or mantra that often emerges as I move on labyrinths?

If I use a labyrinth pattern as a paradigm for understanding life, what do I perceive?

Which labyrinth pattern or patterns resonate most strongly with me right now?

Which shapes embedded in labyrinth patterns speak most evocatively to my imagination?

What factors contribute to the meaningfulness of my labyrinth encounters?

How has the labyrinth facilitated growing integration of my body, mind, and spirit?

From a vantage point outside the labyrinth, what do I perceive about the inside of the labyrinth?

Why do labyrinths help me to find my way?

Is there any significance to the ease with which I lose track of linear time while on the labyrinth?

What experiences of healing have been influenced by my exposure to labyrinths?

How is my life becoming a reflection of my labyrinth experiences?

How do the circular or spiral patterns of labyrinths relate to other circles and spirals that are a part of my life?

What might labyrinths symbolize?

How are my perceptions of labyrinth symbols changing?

How are my understandings of the center of the labyrinth developing?

As I gaze at images of labyrinths, what symbolic possibilities do I see?

What influences do labyrinths have on their surroundings?

What relationships might exist between water and labyrinths?

Where do I imagine or envision new labyrinths being constructed?

What type of relationship have I experienced between the earth and labyrinths?

In what ways can labyrinths be used as tools for reconciliation?

What societal transformations can the labyrinth contribute to?

Where might I help to create a labyrinth?

What do I want others to know about labyrinths?

What questions about labyrinths remain unanswered?

My questions

The marble labyrinth in the floor of the San Vitale
basilica in Ravenna, Italy, during the 1540s. The design
is notable for the clear indication of the intended
direction of movement through the labyrinth.

part four

QUESTIONS TO PONDER

FOR SPECIAL REASONS

Ten

SPIRITUAL EXPLORATION

A playground awaits:
its form—a labyrinth.
Serious work can happen anywhere!

Why am I here?

What are my deepest prayers for the world?

What spiritual truths orient me?

What inspires me?

What are the kindest things that I have done?

If I were to go in for an annual spiritual "checkup," what concerns would I want to have explored?

How is grace unfolding in my life?

What am I being invited to share?

What spiritual longings ache within?

When has compassion touched me?

How are my longings to connect with the Divine inviting me to change?

As my heart leads my body, for whom do I find myself praying?

What embodied experiences of the Sacred have meant the most?

Who has been there for me at critical moments of faith?

If I were to experience unlimited courage, what would shift?

What about forgiveness?

The way in is the way out. The way out is the way in. What questions spring forth as I ponder these labyrinth truths?

My questions

*A local printer published this plan of the Shepherd's Race
turf labyrinth at Sneinton, England, shortly after the
labyrinth was regrettably destroyed in 1797.*

Eleven

HEBREW AND CHRISTIAN SCRIPTURES

Well-worded questions
have been known to reverberate
off the walls of my life
for years.

PONDER

"God who planted the ear, does God not hear? God who formed the eye, does God not see?" Psalm 94:9

"My soul is in anguish. How long, O God, how long?" Psalm 6:3 (NIV)

What will help me "be still, and know [you are] God?" Psalm 46:10

"Who can tell anyone what the future holds?" Ecclesiastes 10:14c

"My God, my God, why have you forsaken me? Why are you so far from helping me, from the words of my groaning?" Psalm 22:1

"Is there anything of which one can say, 'Look! This is something new?'" Ecclesiastes 1:10a (NIV)

"How can you say to your neighbor, 'Let me take the speck out of your eye,' while the log is in your own eye?" Matthew 7:4

"The human spirit will endure sickness; but a broken spirit—who can bear?" Proverbs 18:14

"Were not our hearts burning within us while Jesus was talking to us on the road, while he was opening the scriptures to us?" Luke 24:32

"Who do you say that I [Jesus] am?" Luke 9:20

"Why are you cast down, O my soul, and why are you disquieted within me?" Psalm 42:5a

"Do you not know that your body is a temple of the Holy Spirit within you, which you have from God . . . ?" 1 Corinthians 6:19a

CONSIDER

"Do not say, 'Why were the former days better than these?' For it is not from wisdom that you ask this." Ecclesiastes 7:10

"Shall I not drink the cup God has given me?" John 18:11 (NIV)

"What do you have that you did not receive?" 1 Corinthians 4:7b

Questions from the Scriptures that I would like to add

*The Hopi people of Arizona have two forms
of the labyrinth—the traditional classical style and a
square form known as Tapu'at, with two entrances
that create two labyrinths, one within the other.*

Twelve

SPECIAL DAYS

Today is not like every other day.
Rather than pretend it is,
honor its possibilities.

On a birthday
> What are my hopes for the coming year?

Honoring a significant beginning
> What hopes and fears do I bring to this initiation?

Around the time of a wedding
> How can I share my love with members of my family? Others?
> The world community?

When graduating
> What lies ahead?

On a day when you feel especially alive and awake
> What is the greatest gift of this moment?

On an anniversary
> What dreams will lead me forward?

When celebrating someone else's special day
    What is the greatest gift I can offer?

When leaving on a spiritual pilgrimage
    What am I seeking? What do I need?

During times of uncertainty
    How is my use of the labyrinth giving me confidence in taking the
    next step?

When changing jobs
    How can I honor the work I am doing and who I am becoming?

When returning from a time of retreat
    Who am I becoming?

Marking a significant ending
    What joy and grief am I embodying?

After a death
> What memories comfort me?

Before a funeral
> How can I honor the memory of the person who died?

Before visiting a cemetery
> How can I best express the love I had for the person whose grave I will
> be visiting?

When grief-stricken
> Who can support me? What do I need?

On May Day
> If I were a flower, what would my name be?

At the spring equinox
> What is coming to life within me?

At the summer solstice
  What fullness needs celebration?

At the fall equinox
  How will drawing inward become a gift?

At the winter solstice
  In what ways am I willing to honor both the darkness and the light?

During a full moon
  What quiet beauty is calling to me?

As the moon is waxing
  What is growing?

As the moon is waning
  Am I willing to let go of what is no longer needed?

My questions

A Roman labyrinth mosaic pavement from
Cormérod, Switzerland, has an unusual eight-fold
design and a depiction of Theseus battling the
Minotaur at its goal.

Thirteen

Stoking the Flames of Your Creativity

To get unstuck,

you have to move.

It really is that simple!

When will I be able to take my favorite art supplies to the center of the labyrinth and use them there?

If the only way I could share the beauty of the labyrinth was through dance, what would my first steps be?

Are there notes, sounds, or melodies that I hear again and again as I experience labyrinths? To what are they inviting me?

How will I complete the statement, "As I move on the labyrinth, I can almost taste . . ."

If the smells I've experienced on labyrinths had a voice, what would they ask me to do?

As the labyrinth holds me, what new creation is being nurtured?

How will I care for the seed of a poem, composition, painting, or other creative venture that was planted in me while I was on a labyrinth?

Is there a new labyrinth pattern that wants to be born through me?

What do I need to do to ready myself to create labyrinths?

My questions

*Situated in a clearing deep in the
Eilenriede forest, the Rad turf labyrinth near
Hanover in Germany has a fully grown tree
at the center of its swirling pathways.*

Fourteen

CONSTRUCTING A LABYRINTH

Some people are sure.
"I will never be able to build a labyrinth."

That's what I thought too!

Funny thing,
Four labyrinths I constructed are visible out my window,
in the basement are several large labyrinths I painted,
and long ago I lost count of the arts and crafts labyrinths I've made.

Wait and see.
Anything is possible!

CONCEPTUAL QUESTIONS

Whose fingers crafted the first labyrinth on Earth? What need did it meet?

Archeologists have found labyrinths etched in rocks, imprinted on coins, doodled on manuscripts, and decorating floors, vases, pillars, and ceilings. If money and materials were not a concern, where would I place a labyrinth?

What construction choices have most contributed to my labyrinth experiences? Orientation? Environmental placement? Size? Pattern? Materials?

What do I need to know or do before I will be ready to construct a labyrinth?

What is the story of my favorite labyrinth's conception and gestation? What was my role during its pregnancy?

If I were to construct a labyrinth, what intentions and prayers would support its birth?

Who might be interested in creating a labyrinth with me?

CONSIDERATIONS BEFORE STARTING CONSTRUCTION

Who will use this labyrinth once it is created?

Which labyrinth pattern best suits the needs of those who will come?

What is being communicated through the pattern being chosen?

Will this labyrinth be dedicated to a specific purpose?

What materials will best support the mission of this labyrinth?

Will this labyrinth be temporary or permanent?

What will be placed near the labyrinth to enhance the experiences of those who come?

What blessings shall be offered for this labyrinth and its creators before, during, and after its creation?

My questions

The Shepherd's Race turf labyrinth on Boughton Green,
England, was unfortunately destroyed in 1917.
The curious design had a spiral at the center.

Fifteen

QUESTIONS FOR THE LABYRINTH

Will the labyrinth answer my queries

the way a person might?

No.

Do I still have questions

I would like to ask?

Yes!

Did you find me, did I find you, or did we find each other?

Many call you "Labyrinth." Others, "Troy Town," "Jericho," "Maze," and still others have referred to you as "the Path to Jerusalem." What are your other names? What can they teach me?

What is the relationship between your beauty and my own?

Where did you come from?

What are you communicating?

What are some of the things you symbolize?

Where are you leading?

Which of your invitations am I resisting?

What inner stagnation is your winding pathway loosening?

How might you describe your relationship to me?

If you were a whirlpool, where might I emerge once I had been pulled through your center?

In what ways are you inviting me to share your gifts with others?

Why is "Thank you!" a phrase that bubbles up so often and so naturally when I am with you?

What do I want to communicate to others about you?

How can my efforts on your behalf benefit others?

My questions

*A labyrinthine geoglyph marked during the first few
centuries C.E. on the Nasca plains in Peru. Although not a
true classical labyrinth, the pathway was probably walked
as part of a ceremonial practice.*

RESOURCES

*Questions can lead you
to the most wonderful destinations!*

Deep Haven Labyrinths and Retreats
Jill Kimberly Hartwell Geoffrion
www.jillkhg.com

Labyrinth Enterprises
Robert Ferré, Master Labyrinth Builder
Labyrinth construction and consultation; extensive internet links
128 Slocum, St. Louis, MO 63119
800-873-9873, fax 888-873-9873
www.labyrinth-enterprises.com

The Labyrinth Society
Annual international labyrinth gatherings, regional connections, web
forums and resources, including extensive bibliography
P.O. Box 144, New Canaan, CT 06840-0144
877-446-4520
www.labyrinthsociety.org

Labyrinthos
Jeff and Kimberly Saward, Directors
Labyrinth Resources Centre, photo library & archive; publisher of
Caerdroia—the Journal of Labyrinths and Mazes
53 Thundersley Grove, Thundersley, Essex SS7 3EB England
www.labyrinthos.net

Veriditas, The World Wide Labyrinth Project at Grace Cathedral
Lauren Artress, Founder
Labyrinth events, resources, and international labyrinth locator
1100 California Street, San Francisco, CA 94108
415-749-6358, fax 415-749-6357, TTY 415-749-6359
www.gracecathedral.org/labyrinth

BIBLIOGRAPHY

Give thanks

for those who have gone before . . .

Artress, Lauren. *Walking a Sacred Path: Rediscovering the Labyrinth as a Spiritual Tool.* New York: Riverhead Books, 1995.

Curry, Helen. *The Way of the Labyrinth: A Powerful Meditation for Everyday Life.* New York: Penguin Compass, 2000.

Ferré, Robert. *Church Labyrinths: Questions and Answers Regarding the History, Relevance, and Use of Labyrinths in Churches.* St. Louis: One Way Press, 2001.

Geoffrion, Jill Kimberly Hartwell. *Praying the Labyrinth: A Journal for Spiritual Creativity.* Cleveland: Pilgrim Press, 1999.

————. *Living the Labyrinth: 101 Paths to a Deeper Connection with the Sacred.* Cleveland: Pilgrim Press, 2000.

————. *Labyrinth and the Song of Songs.* Cleveland: Pilgrim Press, 2003.

Geoffrion, Jill Kimberly Hartwell, and Elizabeth Catherine Nagel. *The Labyrinth and the Enneagram: Circling into Prayer.* Cleveland: Pilgrim Press, 2001.

Kern, Hermann. *Through the Labyrinth: Designs and Meanings over 5,000 Years.* New York: Prestel, 2000.

Rodriguez, Rebecca. Labyrinth Meditation Cards. Canyon Lake, TX: Blue Nautilus, 2001. www.surrendertotheheart.com.

Sands, Helen Raphael. *The Healing Labyrinth: Finding Your Path to Inner Peace.* New York: Barrons, 2001.

Saward, Jeff. *Ancient Labyrinths of the World.* Thundersley, England: Caerdroia, 1997.

Saward, Jeff. *Magical Paths: Labyrinths and Mazes in the 21rst Century.* London: Mitchell Beazley, 2002.

Schaper, Donna, and Carole Ann Camp. *Labyrinths from the Outside In.* Woodstock, VT: Skylight Paths Publishing, 2000.

Villette, Jean. *The Enigma of the Labyrinth.* St. Louis: One Way Press, 1995.

West, Melissa Gayle. *Exploring the Labyrinth: A Guide for Healing and Spiritual Growth.* New York: Broadway Books, 2000.

Westbury, Virginia. *Labyrinths: Ancient Paths of Wisdom and Peace.* Sydney, Australia: Lansdowne Publishing, 2001.

Wright, Craig. *The Maze and the Warrior: Symbols in Architecture, Theology and Music.* Cambridge, MA: Harvard University Press, 2001.

Related Titles from The Pilgrim Press

LIVING THE LABYRINTH
101 Paths to a Deeper Connection with the Sacred
JILL KIMBERLY HARTWELL GEOFFRION

This book offers beginners and seasoned labyrinth users a multitude of new ways to approach this sacred tool. The short, devotional-like chapters may be used however the reader chooses—because any way that the labyrinth is approached is a right way.
0-8298-1372-1/104 pages/paper/$17.00

PRAYING THE LABYRINTH
A Journal for Spiritual Exploration
JILL KIMBERLY HARTWELL GEOFFRION

This book is a journal that leads readers into spiritual exercise of self-discovery through scripture selections, journaling questions, and poetry, with generous space for personal reflections.
0-8298-1343-8/128 pages/paper/$15.00

THE LABYRINTH AND THE ENNEAGRAM
Circling into Prayer
JILL KIMBERLY HARTWELL GEOFFRION AND ELIZABETH CATHERINE NAGEL

Gives readers an orientation in the enneagram and an explanation of the nine positions of attention that affect the ways in which we respond to the sacred and to others. Includes exercises on the labyrinth with scripture references.
0-8298-1450-7/128 pages/paper/$15.00

LABYRINTH AND THE SONG OF SONGS

JILL KIMBERLY HARTWELL GEOFFRION

A unique spiritual experience—the fourth in Geoffrion's labyrinth series—cleverly intertwining traditional labyrinthine concepts and the entire Hebrew Scriptures love poem "Song of Songs." This is for the seasoned labyrinth aficionado who wants to take the next step, spiritually speaking. Features illustrations of the labyrinth of Chartres Cathedral in France as well as an original hymn entitled "Circling the Labyrinth."

0-8298-1539-2/112 pages/paper/$12.00

To order these or any other books from The Pilgrim Press call or write to:

The Pilgrim Press
700 Prospect Avenue East
Cleveland, Ohio 44115-1100

PHONE ORDERS: 1-800-537-3394 (M–F, 8:30 AM–4:30 PM ET)

FAX ORDERS: 216-736-2206

Please include shipping charges of $4.00 for the first book and $0.75 for each additional book.

Or order from our web site at www.pilgrimpress.com.

Prices subject to change without notice.